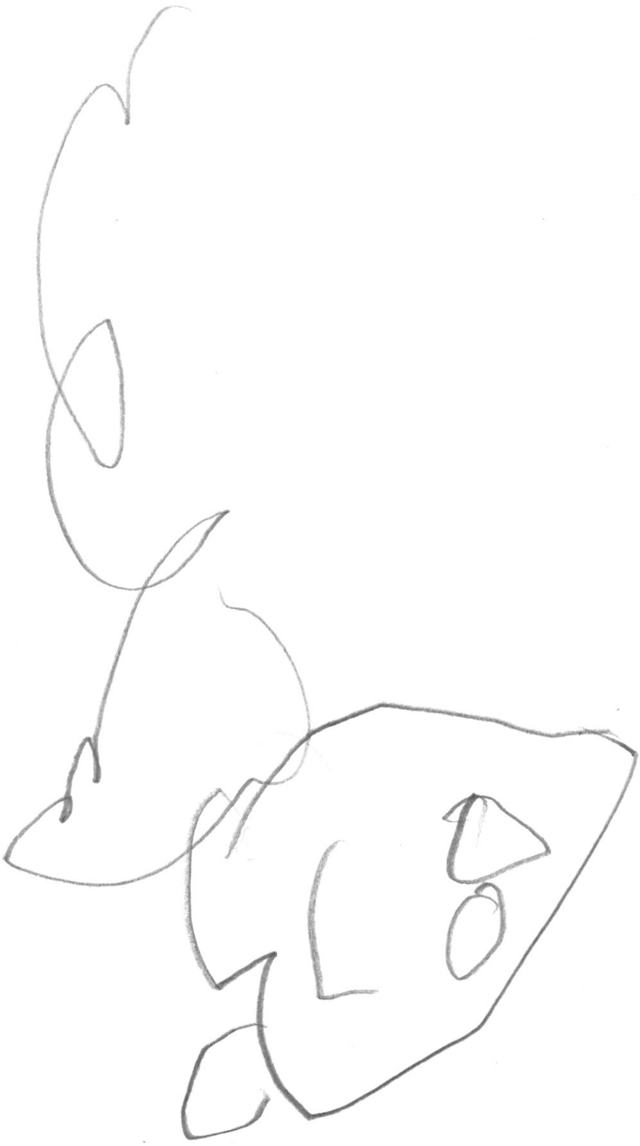

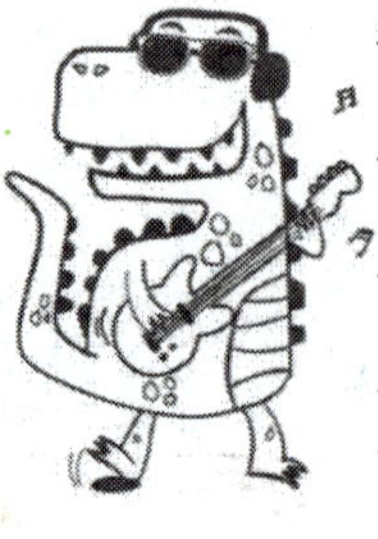

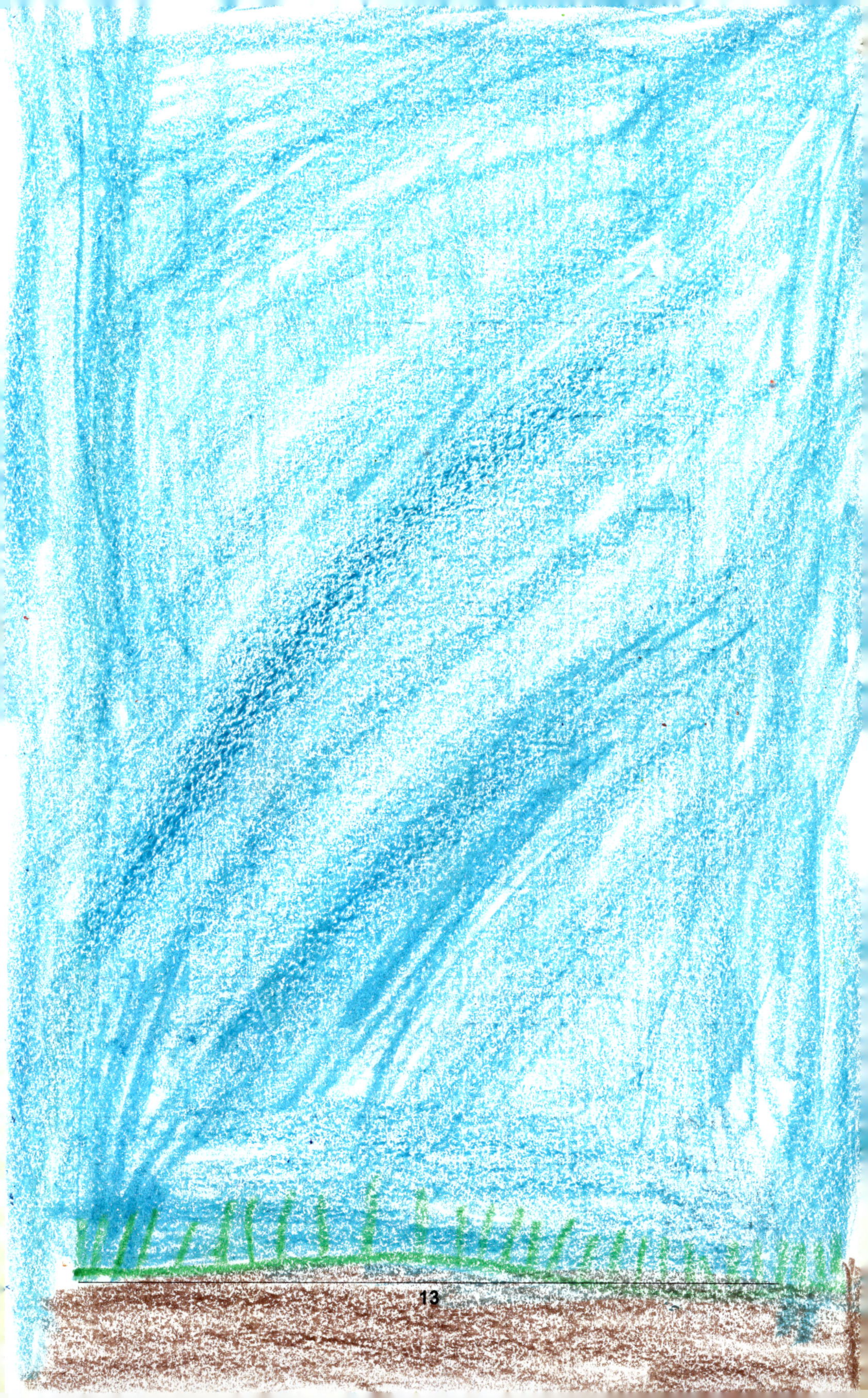

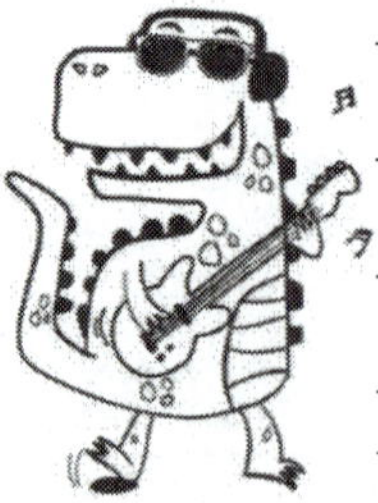

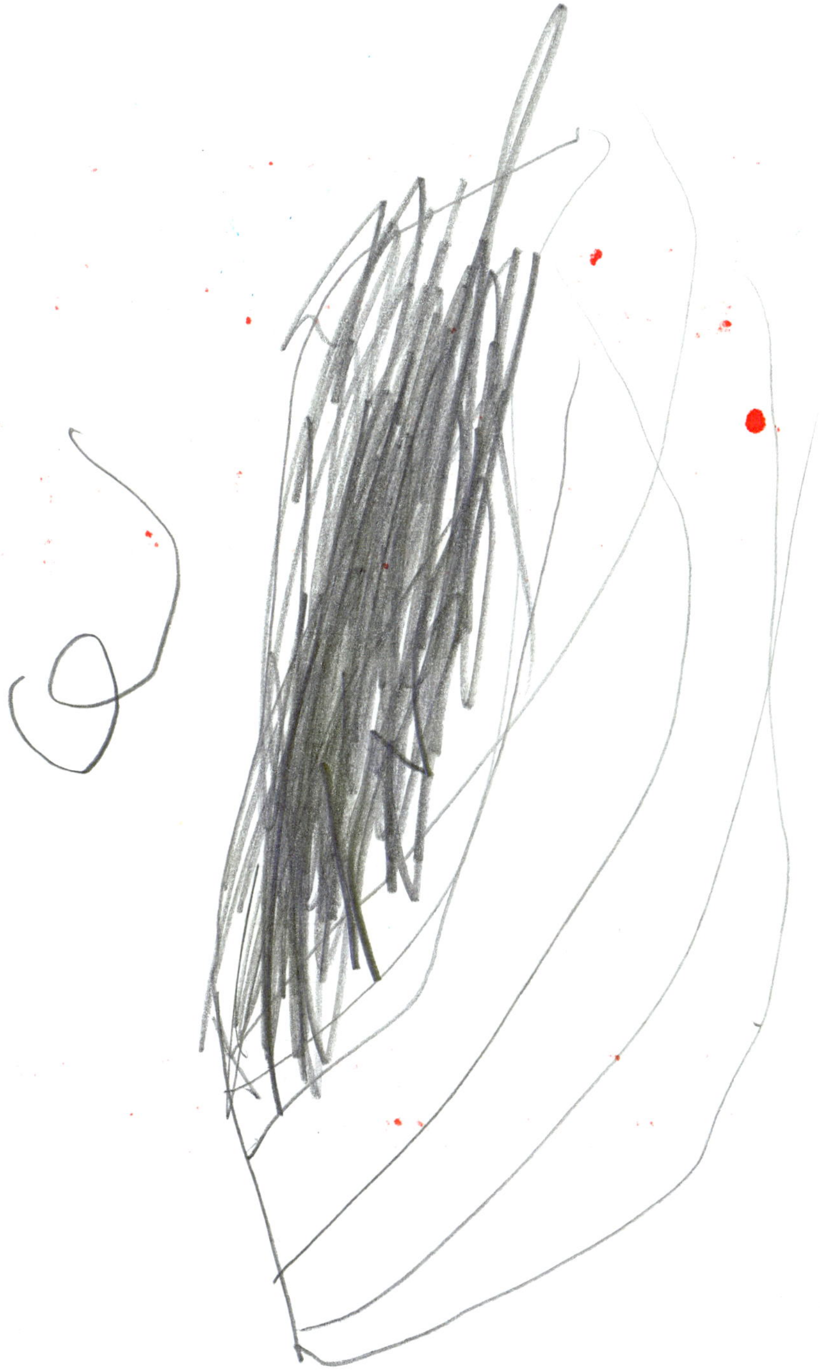

I am sorry that
I haunt your feelings
I am riley sorry

I like how you put all your effert in to makeing the Baby to be born

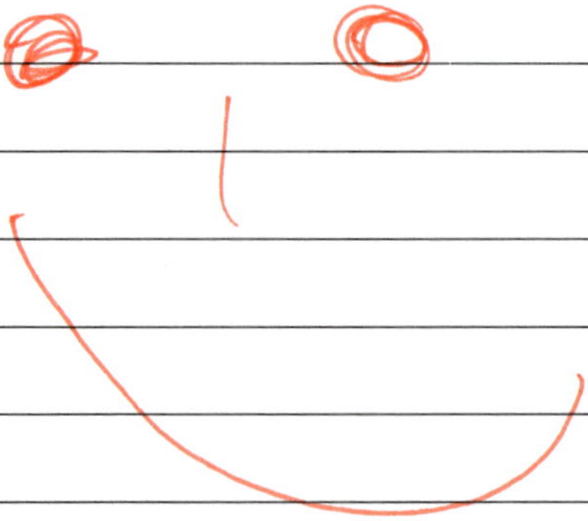

I LOOK forerd to meting You and your Baby cole.

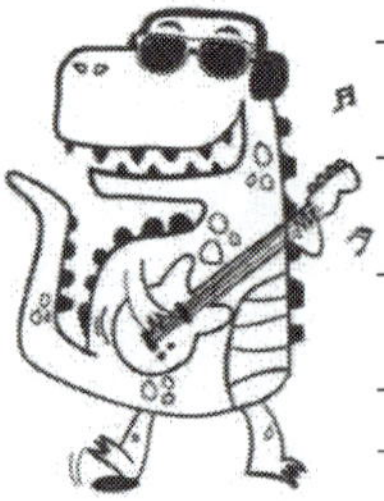

Love, John

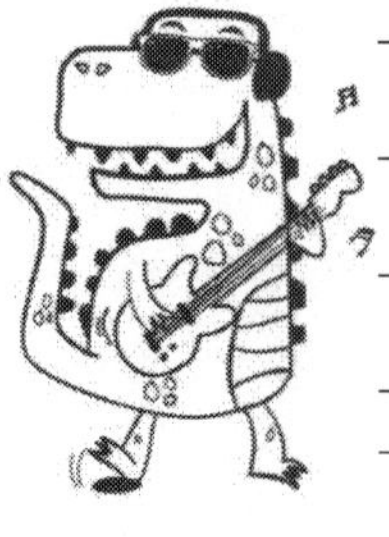

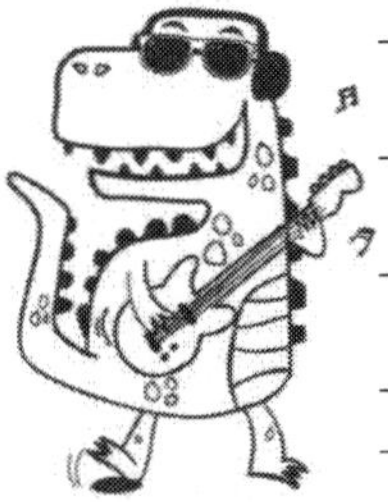

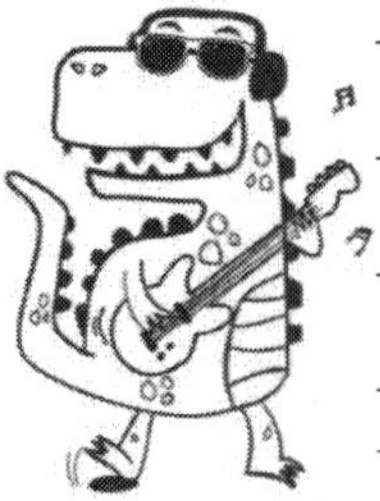

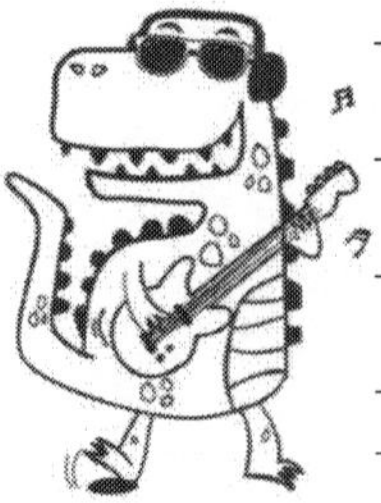

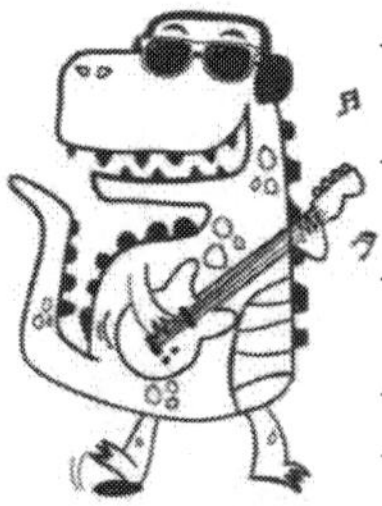

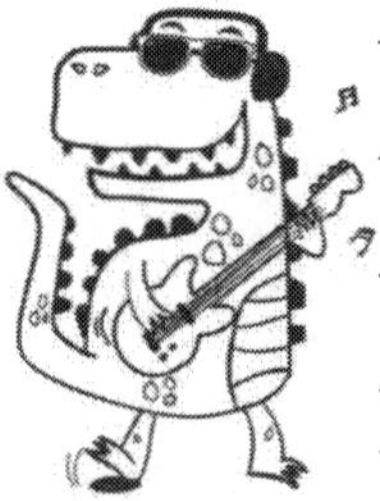

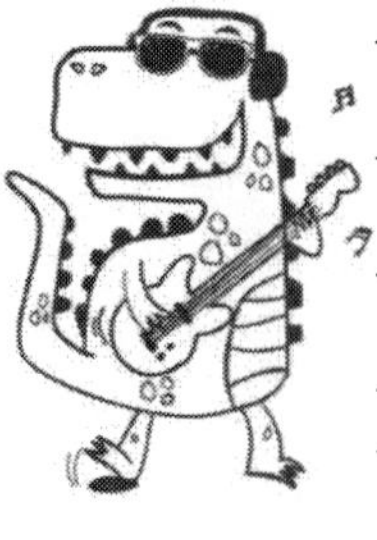

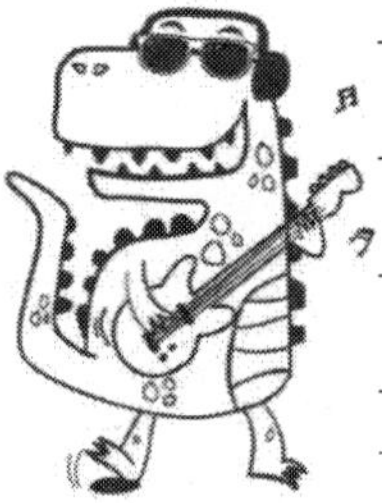

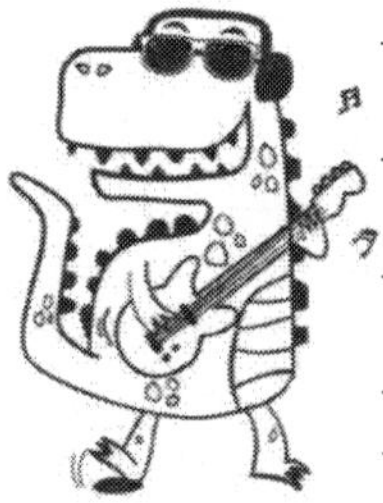

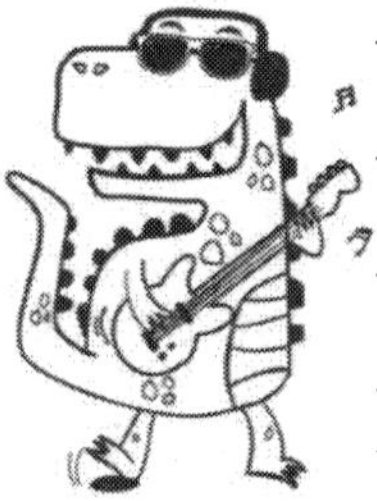

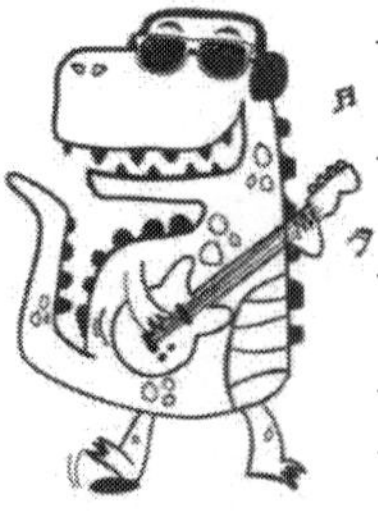

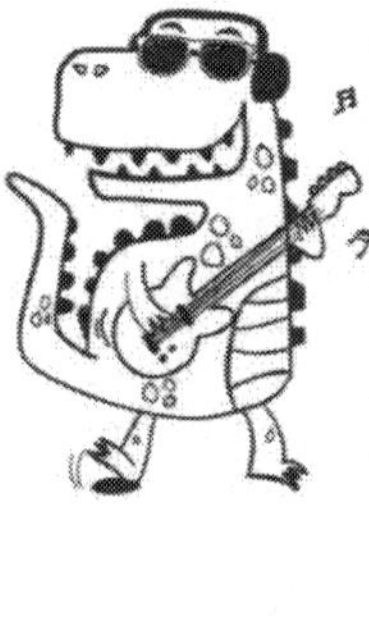

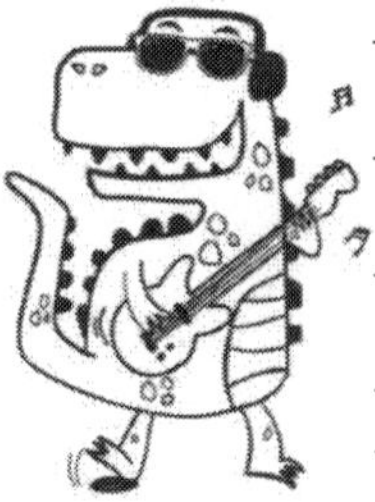

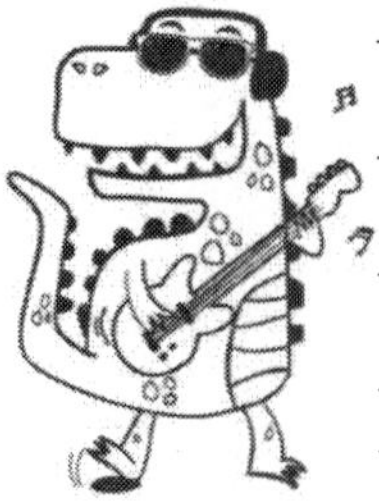

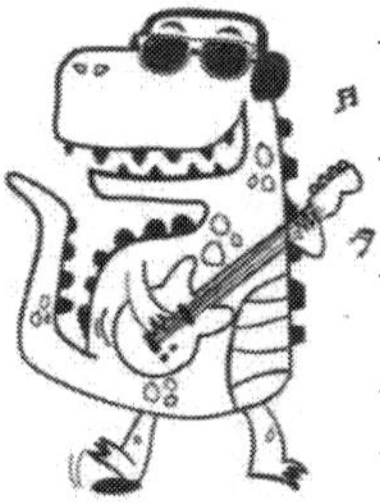

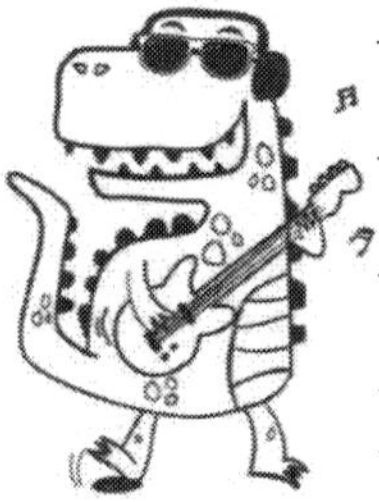

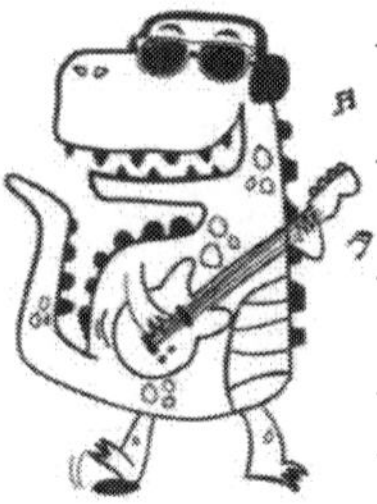

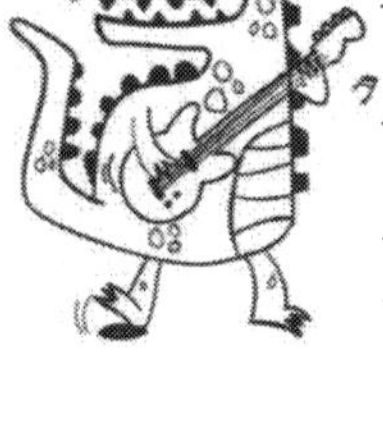

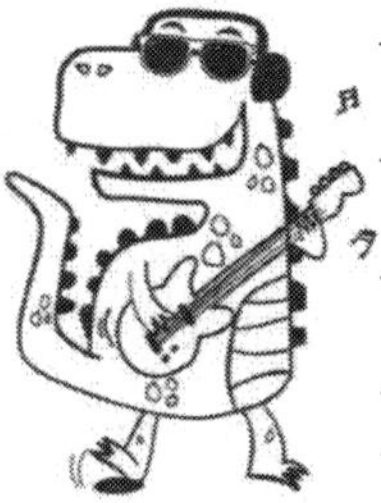

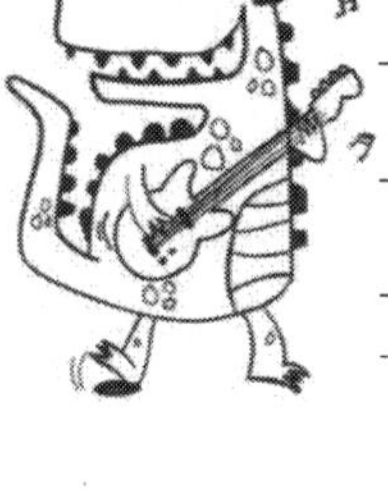

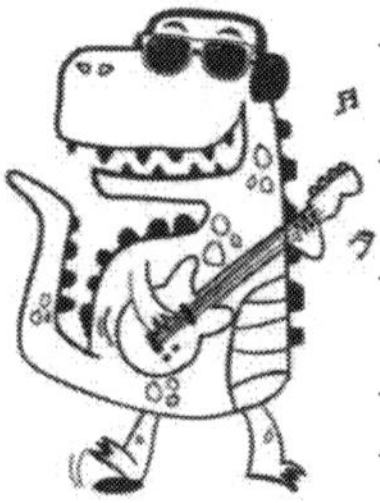

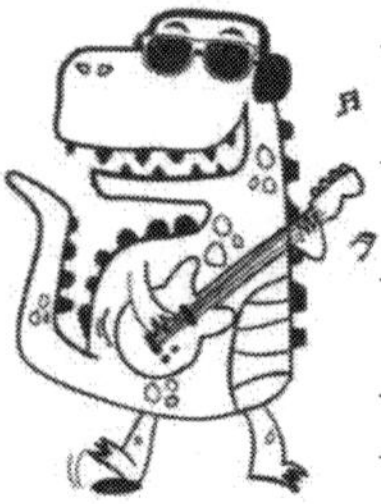

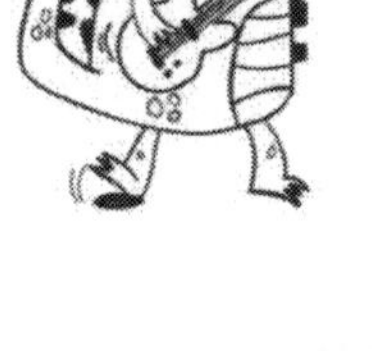

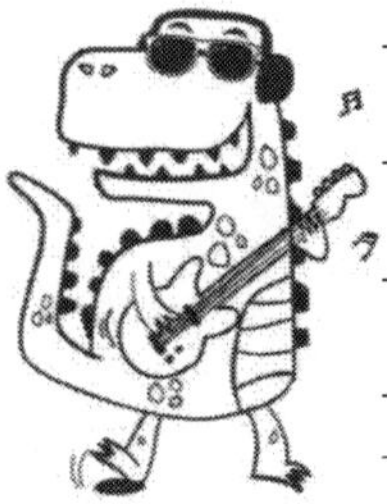

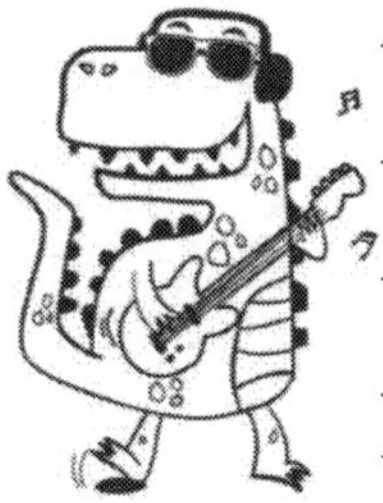

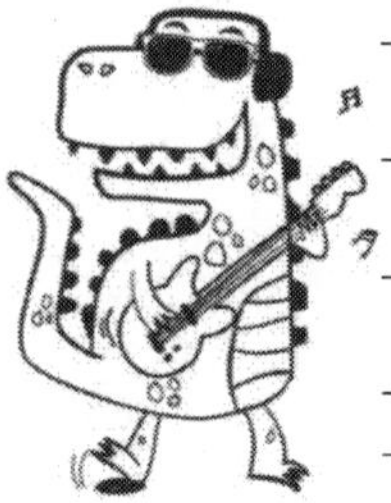

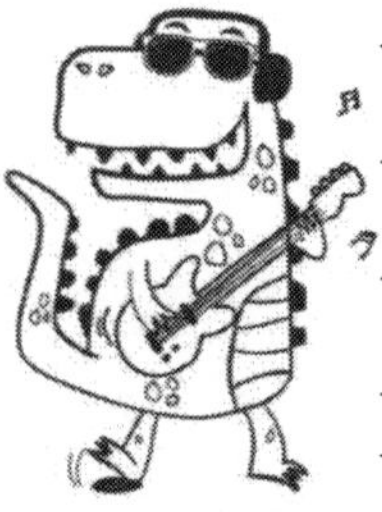

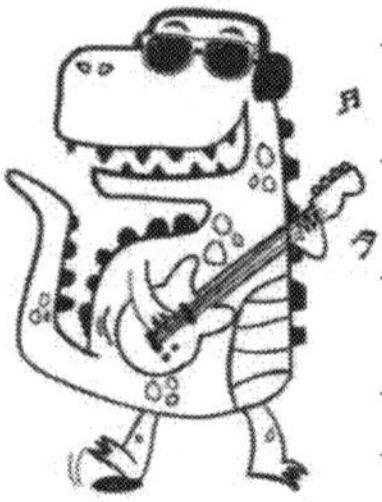

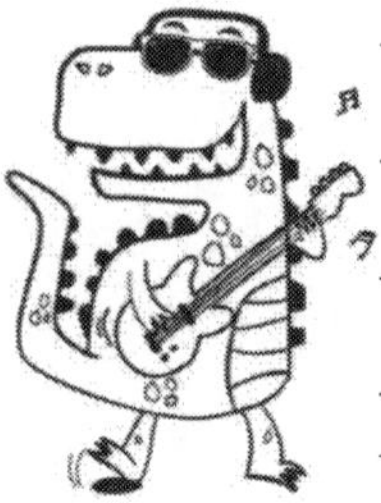

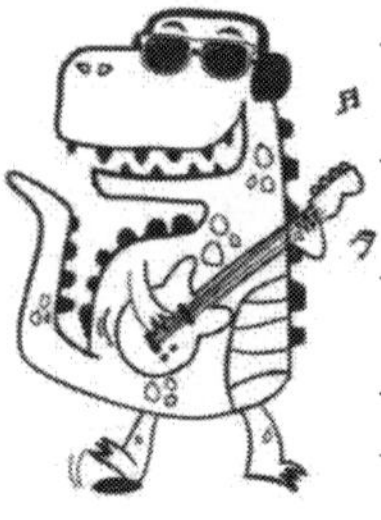

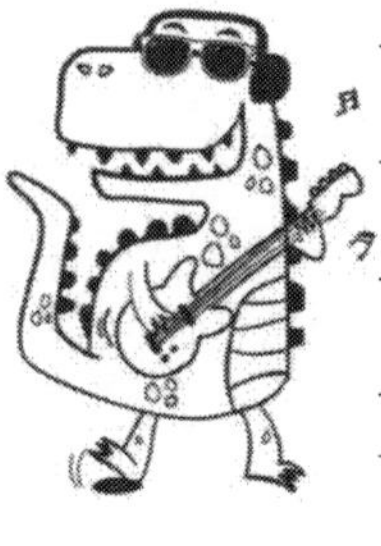

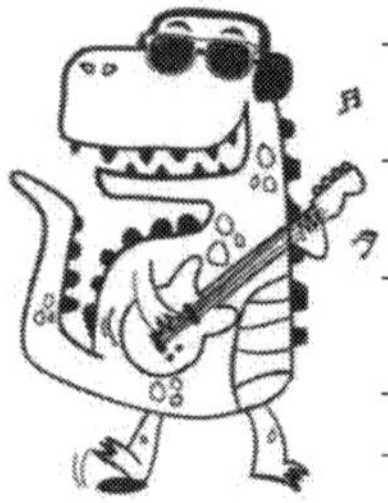

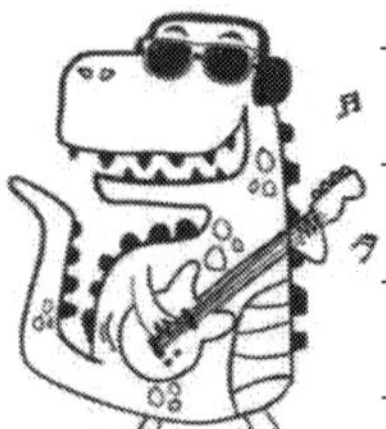

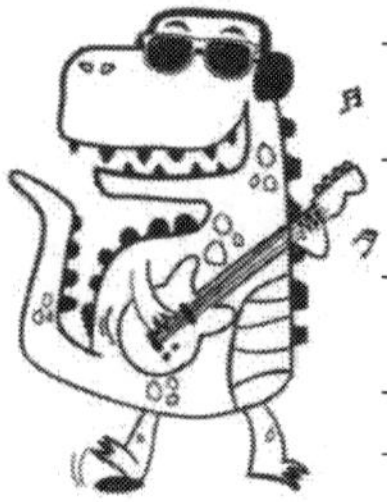

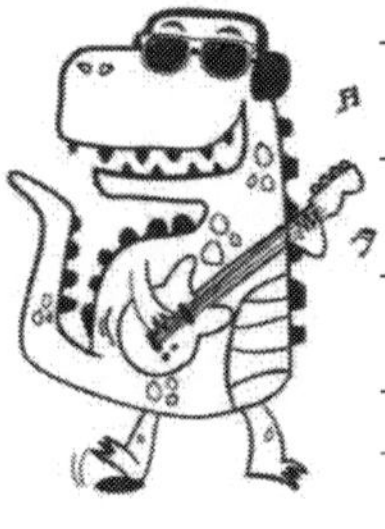

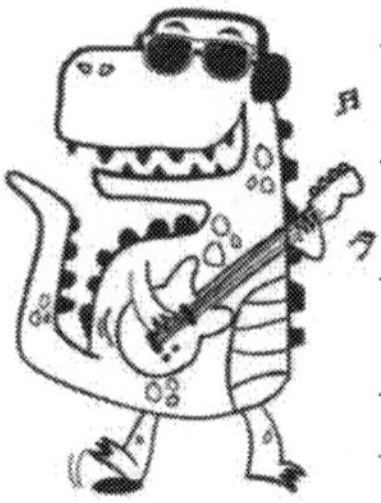

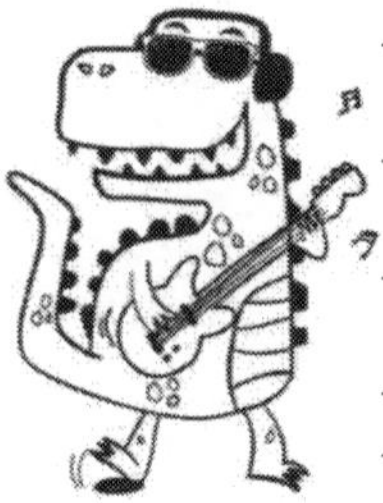

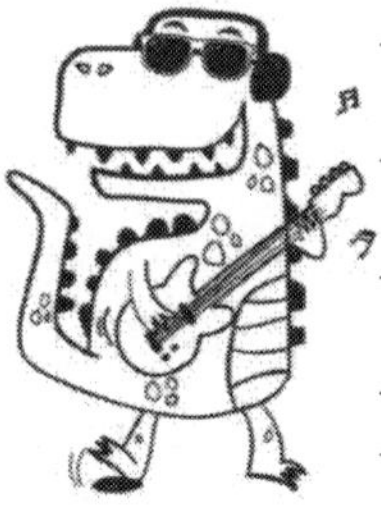

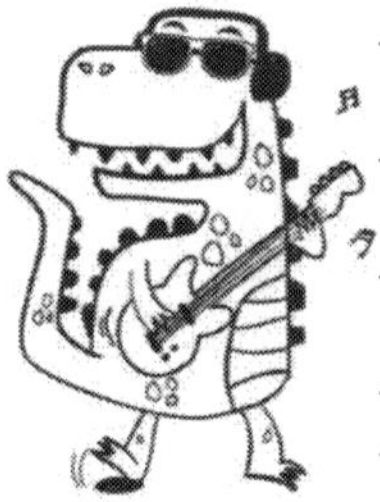

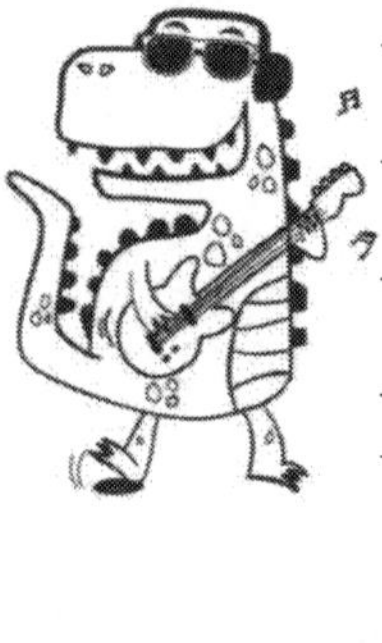

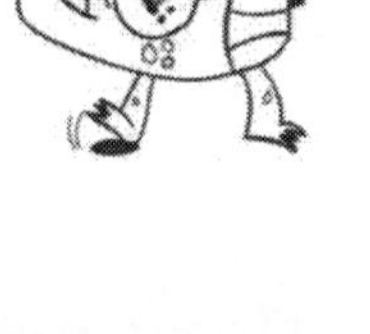

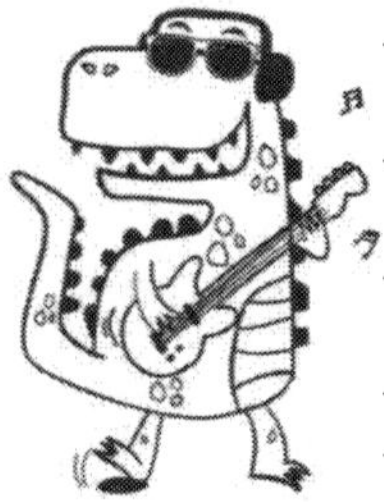

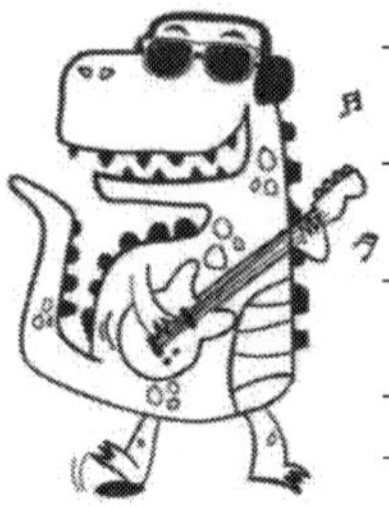

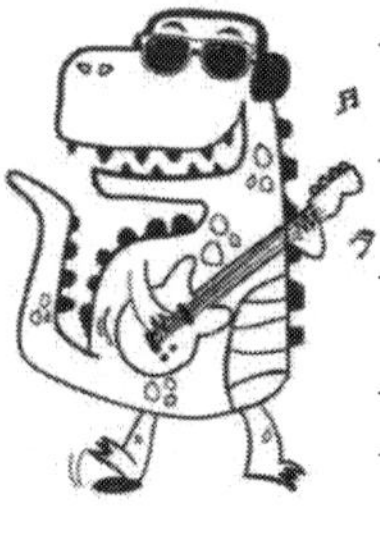

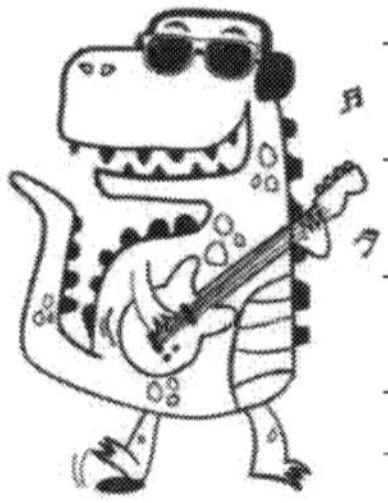

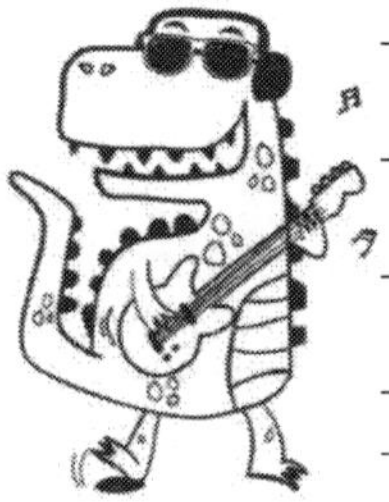

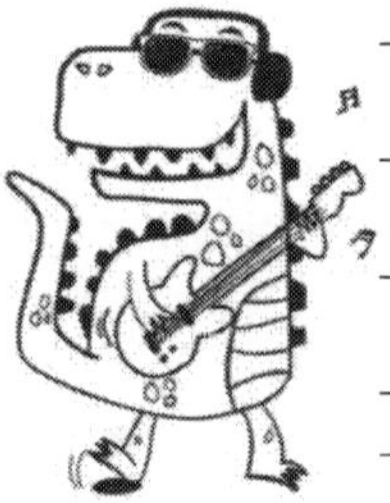

Made in the USA
San Bernardino, CA
02 November 2019

59362940R00062